# THE MEANING OF PRIDE

WRITTEN BY
**ROSIEE THOR**

ILLUSTRATED BY
**SAM KIRK**

 **VERSIFY**

*An Imprint of HarperCollinsPublishers*

BOSTON   NEW YORK

For every member of the LGBTQIA+ community, past, present, and future: your existence makes our world more vibrant and joyful.

And for Jenny Q: you have a way with color, and truly brought it to life in this book.

Versify® is an imprint of HarperCollins Publishers.
Versify is a registered trademark of HarperCollins Publishers LLC.

The Meaning of Pride
Text copyright © 2022 by Rosiee Thor
Illustrations copyright © 2022 by Sam Kirk

The Library of Congress Cataloging-in-Publication Data is on file.
ISBN: 978-0-358-40151-3

The illustrations in this book were created digitally.
The text was set in Avenir.
Cover design by David Hastings
Interior design by David Hastings and Sam Kirk

Manufactured in Italy
RTLO 10 9 8 7 6 5 4 3 2 1
4500841994

First Edition

Every year in June, we celebrate Pride.

Everyone is welcome, whether

LESBIAN

GAY

INTERSEX

ASEXUAL

BISEXUAL  .

TRANS 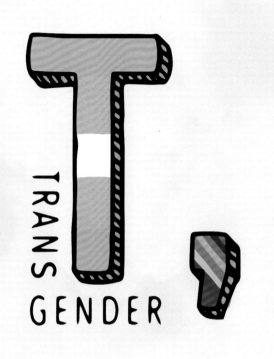 GENDER .

QUEER 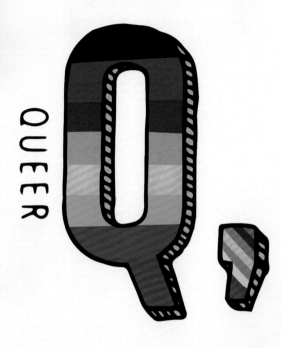 .

PANSEXUAL  .

 AND MORE!

Allies can join in too!

In 1969, members of the LGBTQIA+ community, like Marsha P. Johnson and Stormé DeLarverie, stood up for their rights.

Unfair laws made safe spaces, like the Stonewall Inn in New York City, targets and put their patrons in danger. On June 28, these activists fought back for their community.

EMMA GOLDMAN

AUDRE LORDE

HARVEY MILK

LGBTQIA+ people have been fighting for our rights for a long time.

We've worked hard so that we can all be true to who we are.

To honor the past, present, and future of LGBTQIA+ culture, we march in Pride festivals all around the world that celebrate our community.

# Pride means wearing whatever you want.

BILLY PORTER

LENA WAITHE

If it makes you feel good, it's fierce.

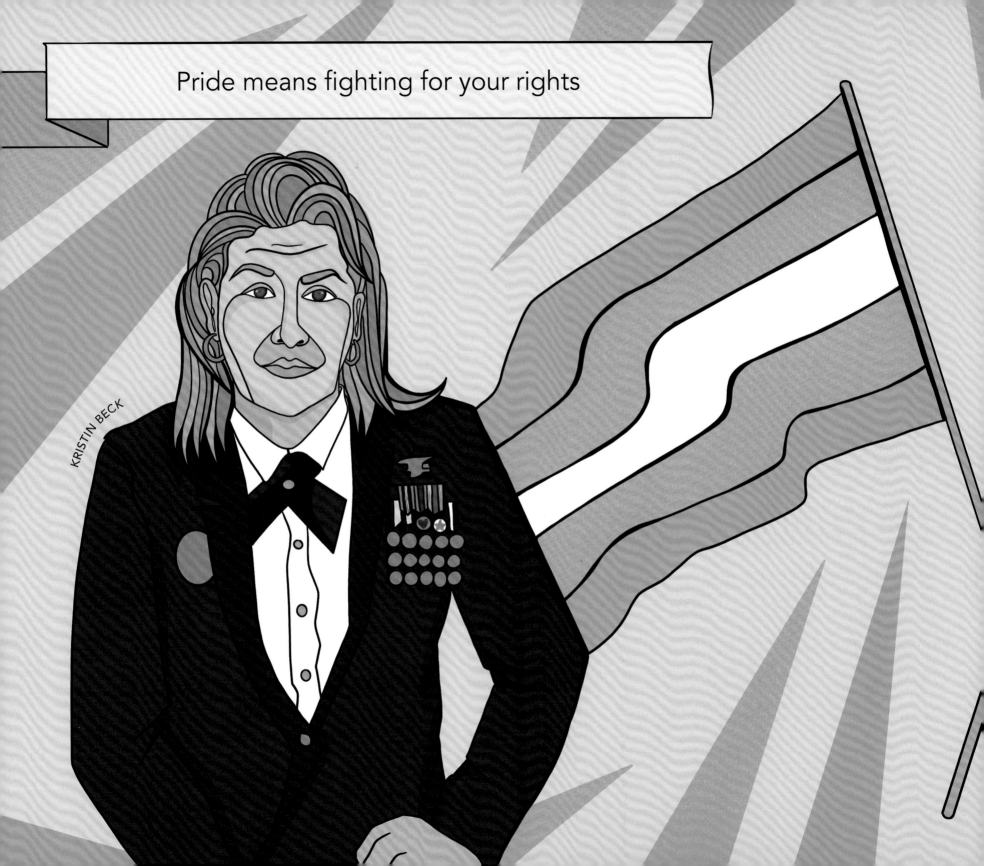

Pride means running
toward a better future

KATE BROWN

GOVERNOR

PROTECT
TRANS

ANDREA JENKINS

CITY COUNCIL

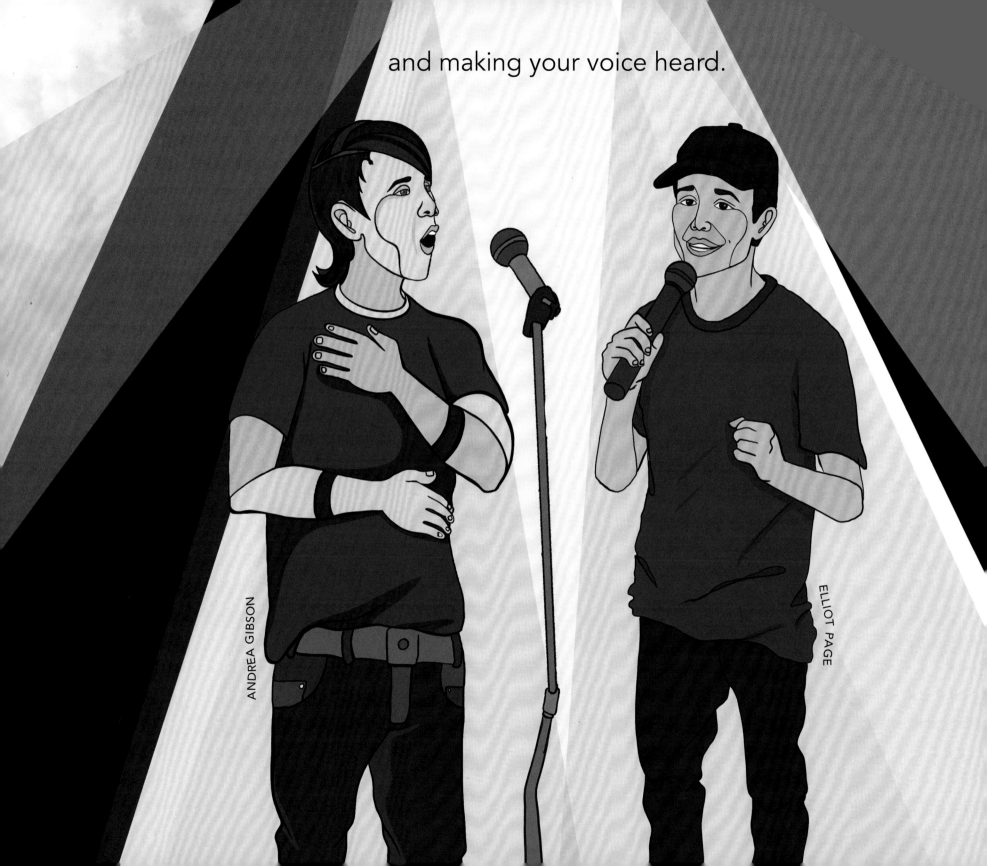

Pride means
living your truth . . .

MATTHEW SHEPARD

ALVIN AILEY

JOSEPHINE BAKER

or dancing it . . .

Pride means taking care of your heart, body, and mind.

is love

MERCEDES SANTOS

THERESA VOLPE

is love.

And most of all, Pride means loving yourself.

What does pride mean to you?

Dear Reader,

Pride is an important feeling—just like happiness, sadness, excitement, and love! This book is about people who are proud of who they are and share that pride with others.

It can be hard to feel proud sometimes, especially when people tell us not to be. For the LGBTQIA+ community, being loud and proud is a big win. That's what pride is all about!

Every June, the LGBTQIA+ community honors the people who fought for our freedom to be who we are. Seeing other people celebrate their identities can help us feel ready to celebrate our own!

Celebrating your identity doesn't have to be public, though. You can celebrate with rainbows and parades, or you can celebrate just by being proud of yourself.

So, Reader, we ask you to be proud. Not just in June, but year-round.

Be proud of your successes, be proud of your skills, be proud of your happiness, and be proud of yourself for who you are.

Pride is not the opposite of being humble. It is the opposite of being ashamed. You deserve to be proud!

Wherever you are in your journey, we are proud of you.

*Rosiee Thor and Sam Kirk*

Dear Adult Reader,

Many of us first encounter the word "pride" as a sin—something we should try not to feel. Now we know that pride is a virtue, too.

A lack of self-esteem can negatively affect the lives of LGBTQIA+ youth, so we hope you'll encourage others to see pride as a positive thing and celebrate LGBTQIA+ people for who they are. Whether you are a parent, a teacher, a librarian, or another adult in a child's life, you can have an impact on how they see themselves.

Educating children about LGBTQIA+ history is a great way to help LGBTQIA+ youth feel included and accepted. It can show them the path their community has taken to get to where we are and encourage them to see a better and brighter future. We hope this book contributes to this education and shows them they are not alone.

To help you and your child explore more about LGBTQIA+ history, we have included some recommended reading about some of the people included in this book.

Happy reading, and happy Pride!

*Rosiee Thor and Sam Kirk*

## To Learn More

*I Am Perfectly Designed* by Karamo Brown

*Pride: The Story of Harvey Milk and the Rainbow Flag* by Rob Sanders

*When You Look Out the Window: How Phyllis Lyon and Del Martin Built a Community* by Gayle E. Pitman

People of Pride series by Little Bee Books

Little People, Big Dreams series by Maria Isabel Sánchez Vegara

## Biographies

The public figures in this book are just a small sample of the LGBTQIA+ community. We wanted to include a wide variety of famous people—from politicians to singers to actors to activists—as well as LGBTQIA+ people of different races and identities.

The LGBTQIA+ community is not just one thing or one type of person, and it is important to us to acknowledge the intersectionality of the community. Representation matters a great deal, especially to marginalized youth, and seeing themselves in others can make a difference.

The information about the public figures included in this book is up to date as of publication; however, we know the words and pronouns we use to describe our identities can change. For many of us, discovering and communicating our identities is a journey. Additionally, this text is not intended as an endorsement of any of the individuals depicted.

ALVIN AILEY (1931–89) (he/him) was a gay, Black American dancer and choreographer, who founded Alvin Ailey American Dance Theater. He died from an AIDS-related illness.* (p. 26)

SEIMONE AUGUSTUS (she/her) is a lesbian, Black American basketball player. She played for and now coaches the Los Angeles Sparks in the WNBA and is an eight-time all-star. (p. 18)

JOSEPHINE BAKER (1906–75) (she/her) was a bisexual, Black American, France-based dancer, entertainer, and activist. Her image has become an iconic symbol of the roaring twenties. (p. 26)

JAMES BALDWIN (1924–87) (he/him) was a gay, Black American writer and activist for civil rights. He was the author of *Giovanni's Room*, *If Beale Street Could Talk*, and more. (p. 13)

KRISTIN BECK (she/her) is a decorated, white American former Navy SEAL, the first openly transgender former SEAL in American history. (p. 22)

KARAMO BROWN (he/him) is an Emmy-nominated, gay, Black American TV personality and activist. He is best known for his role as the culture expert on the reboot of *Queer Eye*. (p. 31)

KATE BROWN (she/her) is a bisexual white American and the governor of Oregon. She became the first openly queer US-state secretary of state in 2009 and governor in 2015. (p. 24)

RUPAUL CHARLES (he/him) is an Emmy-winning, Black American drag queen known for his music, personality, and popular drag competition show, *RuPaul's Drag Race*. (p. 17)

SHEA COULEÉ (they/them) is a gay, nonbinary, Black American drag queen. They were a finalist on season 9 of *RuPaul's Drag Race* and won season 5 of *RuPaul's Drag Race All Stars*. (p. 31)

LAVERNE COX (she/her) is an Emmy-winning, transgender, Black American actress and activist. She is the first openly transgender actress to play an openly transgender TV series regular. (p. 21)

WILSON CRUZ (he/him) is a gay, Black American actor and activist of Puerto Rican descent, known for roles in the Broadway cast of *Rent*, *My So-Called Life*, and *Star Trek: Discovery*. (p. 20)

LEA DELARIA (she/her) is a gay, white American comedian and actress known for her role in *Orange Is the New Black*. In 1993, she became the first openly gay comedian on American TV. (p. 31)

STORMÉ DELARVERIE (1920–2014) (pronouns varied) was a lesbian, biracial American entertainer and activist credited with helping to spark the Stonewall riots after being attacked by police. (p. 10)

ANDREA GIBSON (they/them) is a nonbinary, white American poet and activist. Their spoken word poetry often touches on LGBTQIA+ themes and topics like gender, identity, and social change. (p. 25)

EMMA GOLDMAN (1869–1940) (she/her) was a white, Russian Jewish immigrant to the United States. She was an advocate for gay rights, feminism, and the anarchist movement. (p. 12)

MISS MAJOR GRIFFIN-GRACY (she/her) is a transgender, Black American activist. She was one of the leaders of the Stonewall uprising in 1969 and an advocate during the AIDS crisis. (p. 13)

ANDREA JENKINS (she/her) is a transgender, Black American politician. In 2018, she became the first openly transgender Black woman elected to public office in the United States. (p. 24)

ELTON JOHN (he/him) is a Grammy-, Oscar-, and Tony-winning, gay, white British musician, songwriter, and composer. He supports gay rights and raises money to fight against AIDS. (p. 27)

MARSHA P. JOHNSON (1945–1992) (pronouns varied) was a Black American drag queen and activist best known for involvement in the Stonewall riots and cofounding the Street Transvestite Action Revolutionaries. (p. 10)

LESLIE JORDAN (he/him) is an Emmy-winning, gay, white American actor and comedian, best known for his role as Beverley Leslie in *Will & Grace* and for his viral social media videos. (p. 31)

FRIDA KAHLO (1907–54) (she/her) was a bisexual, Mexican painter known for her portraits and unique personal image. Her likeness has become iconic in modern fashion, art, and culture. (p. 21)

AUDRE LORDE (1934–92) (she/her) was a lesbian, Black American poet and activist who wrote about injustice, homophobia, sexism, racism, disability, and classism in America. (p. 12)

DEMI LOVATO (they/them) is a Grammy-nominated, American singer of Mexican descent. They identify as queer and are outspoken about their experience with mental health. (p. 28)

PHYLLIS LYON (1924–2020) (she/her) and DEL MARTIN (1921–2008) (she/her) were a white American, lesbian couple and cofounders of the first US national organization for lesbian advocacy. In 2004, they were the first same-sex couple legally married in San Francisco. (p. 29)

RICKY MARTIN (he/him) is a Grammy-winning, gay, Puerto Rican pop musician and humanitarian activist known as the "King of Latin Pop." (p. 27)

FREDDIE MERCURY (1946–91) (he/him) was a bisexual, Indian Parsi British musician and the lead singer of the successful rock band Queen. He died from an AIDS-related illness.* (p. 27)

HARVEY MILK (1930–78) (he/him) was a white American politician, the first openly gay politician in California. He was murdered by a political rival for his gay rights advocacy. (p. 12)

FAWZIA MIRZA (she/her) is a lesbian, Pakistani Canadian actress and comedian. She is best known for creating intersectional work that highlights her identity as a lesbian, Muslim woman. (p. 31)

JANET MOCK (she/her) is a multiracial American, transgender activist and *New York Times* best-selling author. She is the first transgender woman of color to write for a TV series (*Pose*). (p. 31)

JANELLE MONÁE (she/they) is a Grammy-nominated, bisexual/pansexual, Black American singer, songwriter, and actress best known for her roles in *Moonlight* and *Hidden Figures*. (p. 27)

ELLIOT PAGE (he/they) is an Oscar-nominated, transgender, white Canadian actor known for roles in *Juno*, the *X-Men* films, and *The Umbrella Academy* TV series. (p. 25)

**BILLY PORTER** (he/him) is a Tony- and Emmy-winning, Black American actor best known for his roles in *Kinky Boots* and *Pose* and for his gender-nonconforming looks on the red carpet. (p. 16)

**ZACHARY QUINTO** (he/him) is a gay, white American activist and actor best known for his role as Spock in the 2009 movie *Star Trek*. (p. 20)

**SARA RAMIREZ** (she/they) is a Tony-winning, bisexual, nonbinary, Mexican American actor known for her role on *Grey's Anatomy*, the longest-running US prime-time medical drama series. (p. 31)

**MEGAN RAPINOE** (she/her) is a decorated, lesbian, white American professional soccer player and activist. In 2019, she led the US women's soccer team to victory in the World Cup. (p. 18)

**ANTHONY RAPP** (he/him) is a gay, white American actor. He was one of the first openly gay men on Broadway, known for roles in *Rent* and as the first openly gay *Star Trek* TV character. (p. 20)

**ADAM RIPPON** (he/him) is a gay, white American figure skater and Olympian. In 2018, he won a bronze medal, becoming the first openly gay American to medal at the Winter Olympics. (p. 19)

**SYLVIA RIVERA** (1951–2002) (she/her) was an American drag queen and activist of Puerto Rican and Venezuelan descent who cofounded the Street Transvestite Action Revolutionaries. (p. 23)

**MJ RODRIGUEZ** (she/her) is a transgender, biracial American actress known for roles in *Pose* and *Luke Cage*. She played the first transgender character in the Marvel Cinematic Universe. (p. 17)

**MERCEDES SANTOS** (she/her) and **THERESA VOLPE** (she/her) are a lesbian, interracial American couple best known for advocating for LGBTQIA+ families and same-sex marriage rights. They were one of the first same-sex couples to be legally married in the state of Illinois in 2014. (p. 30)

**MATTHEW SHEPARD** (1976–98) (he/him) was a gay, white American student who was murdered in 1998. The Matthew Shepard Act now designates crimes committed on the basis of sexual orientation as hate crimes. (p. 26)

**CHRISTIAN SIRIANO** (he/him) is a gay, white American fashion designer. He is best known for becoming the youngest winner of *Project Runway* in 2008 and for coining the term "fierce." (p. 17)

**SAM SMITH** (they/them) is a gay and genderqueer, white British, Grammy- and Oscar-winning singer and songwriter. (p. 27)

**KRISTEN STEWART** (she/her) is a bisexual, white American actress best known for her starring role as Bella Swan in the *Twilight* film franchise, which broke international box-office records. (p. 28)

**WANDA SYKES** (she/her) is an Emmy-winning, lesbian, Black American actress and comedian known for roles in *Curb Your Enthusiasm*, *Black-ish*, and *The Wanda Sykes Show*. (p. 31)

**TECIA TORRES** (she/her) is a lesbian, American UFC mixed martial artist of Puerto Rican and Portuguese descent. She is engaged to fellow MMA fighter Raquel Pennington. (p. 19)

**LENA WAITHE** (she/her) is an Emmy-winning, lesbian, Black American writer, producer, and actress. A queer fashion icon, she is outspoken about being a Black lesbian in Hollywood. (p. 16)

**OSCAR WILDE** (1854–1900) (he/him) was a celebrated, white Irish author best known for his novel *The Picture of Dorian Gray*. He served a two-year sentence for his sexuality from 1895 to 1897. (p. 13)

**EVAN RACHEL WOOD** (she/her) is an Emmy-nominated, bisexual, white American actress known for roles in *True Blood* and *Westworld* and for advocacy for victims of domestic abuse. (p. 28)

*The HIV/AIDS crisis emerged in the United States during the 1980s. Misconceptions about the disease contributed to homophobia. Many lives were lost to the disease and homophobic violence. Now people affected by HIV/AIDS can live a long time thanks to modern medicine, but stereotypes still continue to impact the LGBTQIA+ community today.